A Healthy Diet

A Healthy Diet

Elaine Landau

Watts LIBRARY™

Franklin Watts
A Division of Scholastic Inc.
New York • Toronto • London • Auckland • Sydney
Mexico City • New Delhi • Hong Kong
Danbury, Connecticut

For Sara Sutin

Note to readers: Definitions for words in **bold** can be found in the Glossary at the back of this book.

Photographs © 2003: Corbis Images/Nathan Benn: 5 bottom left, 31; Dembinsky Photo Assoc./Mark E. Gibson: 38; Envision: 22 (MAK Studio), 16 (George Mattei), 13, 14 (Steven Needham), 5 top left, 11 (Photononstop), 21 (RESO); Getty Images: 8 (C Squared Studios), 27 (Jules Frazier); The Image Bank/Getty Images: 45; Peter Arnold Inc./Jodi Jacobson: cover, 26; Photo Researchers, NY: 29 (Mark C. Burnett), 20 (Richard Hutchings), 6 (Ken Lax); PhotoEdit: 32, 40, 42 (Myrleen Ferguson Cate), 48 (Tony Freeman), 18 (Bonnie Kamin), 46 (David Kelly Crow), 34 (David Urbina), 5 right, 9, 46 (Susan Van Etten), 2, 28, 37, 44 (David Young-Wolff); Visuals Unlimited/D. Yeske: 24.

The photograph on the cover shows a well-balanced meal. The photograph opposite the title page shows a young man taking a bite out of a peach, which is part of a healthy diet.

Library of Congress Cataloging-in-Publication Data

Landau, Elaine.
    A healthy diet / by Elaine Landau
        p. cm. — (Watts library)
    Summary: Explains the different foods and nutrients needed for good nutrition and discusses related health issues.
Includes bibliographical references and index.
    ISBN 0-531-12027-9 (lib. bdg.)   0-531-16668-6 (pbk.)
    1. Nutrition—Juvenile literature. 2. Food—Juvenile literature. [1. Nutrition. 2. Food.] I. Title. II. Series.
TX355 .L23 2003
613.2—dc21

            2002008477

Contents

People need to eat every day. However, not everyone has a healthy diet.

Chapter One

Necessary Nutrients

Regardless of your age, where you live, or what your favorite foods are, you have something in common with everyone else on the planet. Everyone needs **nutrients** to carry on the process of day-to-day living. Nutrients are substances found in foods. They nourish your body, which enables you to grow and fight off disease and infection. The food you eat is broken down into nutrients during **digestion**, which is the process of breaking down food in the body. These nutrients are

Recommended Daily Allowance (RDA)

When you look at food labels, you may see the term **Recommended Daily Allowance** (RDA). This allowance represents the amount of a nutrient most people need.

Some labels now may show Daily Reference Intake (DRI) amounts instead of RDA. The DRI expands on the RDA and includes daily calorie needs.

absorbed into the bloodstream and carried to the various cells of the body.

The human body cannot manufacture most nutrients. They have to come from an outside source. To get all the nutrients necessary for good health, you need to eat a balanced diet. This is a diet consisting of the right amounts of a variety of foods.

A medium-sized apple has about 65 calories.

Food does more than keep you alive. It provides energy for walking, running, and playing sports. The amount of energy that various foods contain is measured in units called **calories**. Different foods have different caloric values. A medium-sized apple contains about 65 calories. One cup of butter pecan ice cream has nearly 500 calories. The average fifth to seventh grader needs to eat about 2,200 calories a day. Sometimes people eat more calories than they use for fuel. These extra calories are stored in the body as **fat**.

Meet the Macronutrients

The nutrients needed for good health are divided into six main groups. Out of these nutrient groups, four are known as **macronutrients**. The human body needs sizable amounts of macronutrients. They are essential for growth, development, repairing body tissues, and energy. The four macronutrients are water, **carbohydrates**, **proteins**, and fats.

Water has been called the overlooked nutrient. Many people are concerned about getting enough protein, but few worry about drinking enough water. Water is an essential nutrient, however. Humans can live for several weeks without food, but they can survive only a few days without water.

Water is an essential part of your diet.

Water is a big part of who you are. More than 60 percent of your body mass is water. The body's cells, tissues, and organs need water to function. The body depends on water to act as its transportation system. As a part of the blood, water carries essential nutrients to cells and flushes out waste from the cells. As urine, it carries certain waste products out of the body.

Water protects parts of the body. The spinal cord, eyes, and brain are all cushioned by a protective layer of water.

9

Water also helps regulate body temperature. This happens when you sweat. Hot water, in the form of perspiration, **evaporates** from your skin. This cools the body and helps keep your body temperature within a very narrow range.

There is no set requirement for how much water a person should drink every day. A person's need for water varies according to climate, physical activity level, age, overall health, and body size. For most individuals, eight 8-ounce (227-milliliter) cups of water a day will do. To avoid **dehydration**—a dangerous depletion of body fluids—it is best to drink water throughout the day. Don't wait until you are thirsty. By then, your body is already missing too much of what it needs.

Carbohydrates

The second group of macronutrients is called carbohydrates, which are also known as starches and sugars. Carbohydrates are found in a remarkable variety of foods. The majority of them come from the starchy parts of plants we eat. You can find carbohydrates in carrots, apples, rice, orange juice, milk, yogurt, and lots of other foods.

The body breaks down starches and sugars into a substance called glucose, which is a type of sugar. After entering the bloodstream, glucose is carried to the body's cells. It serves as an important source of immediate energy.

Carbohydrates are divided into two groups—complex carbohydrates and simple carbohydrates. Complex carbohydrates are starches. Foods containing starch include pasta, bread, and

potatoes. The body breaks down complex carbohydrates slowly, and this provides energy over several hours. Complex carbohydrates keep your energy level on an even keel.

Carbohydrates are found in many different types of food.

Simple carbohydrates consist of sugars. They are found in foods such as honey, maple syrup, cookies, candies, cake, milk, fruit, and fruit juices. The body breaks down simple carbohydrates quickly. Your blood sugar level peaks, and you feel a burst of energy. This energy does not last throughout the day, though.

Not all sugars are the same. Natural sugars, such as those in fruit, can be beneficial. Added sugars, which are sugars and syrups that have been artificially added to foods, are more harmful. Foods with added sugars, such as soda and candy, are usually high in calories and low in essential nutrients. Eating too much of these foods can lead to weight gain.

Proteins

The third essential macronutrient is protein. Proteins exist in every cell of the body. They are complex substances made up of smaller units known as **amino acids**. Humans need an adequate supply of twenty amino acids. The body can produce eleven of these on its own, but nine other amino acids—known as essential amino acids—must come from food.

Proteins that contain adequate levels of all the essential amino acids are called complete proteins. These proteins are found in foods such as cheese, eggs, fish, meats, and milk. Incomplete proteins are proteins that lack at least one essential amino acid. Among the foods containing incomplete proteins are cereal **grains**, vegetables, **legumes**, and nuts. In some cases, two incomplete proteins can be combined to yield the right balance of amino acids. A good example of this is the popular Caribbean dish rice and beans. Another example can

be found in lunch boxes across the United States: peanut butter sandwiches.

Protein can be found in food from animals and in some plant products, such as beans.

Proteins perform several extremely important functions in the human body. They help build new body tissues and repair worn ones. They play a valuable role in maintaining muscles, bones, teeth, blood, and other bodily fluids. Proteins are also key in forming **antibodies** that fight disease and infection.

Proteins known as **enzymes** speed up important chemical reactions, such as digestion. Many **hormones** are also proteins. Hormones are substances in the body that regulate

A Fitting Name

The word *protein* comes from a Greek word meaning "of first importance."

important body processes, such as growth and development. Like carbohydrates, proteins provide the body with energy. People who do not get enough protein experience a lack of energy, stunted growth, and other health problems.

Fats

Here are three examples of fats: butter, vegetable shortening, and oil.

Fats are the final type of macronutrient. While too much fat in a diet is unhealthy, it is still important to your body. Like carbohydrates and proteins, fats provide and store fuel for energy. Fats also travel in the bloodstream transporting **vitamins**, such as A, D, E, and K, through the body. Fats protect the body as well. They form membranes around cells, cushion some organs, and keep the body warm.

There are different types of fats in foods. As shown below, some are better choices than others to include in your diet.

- **Saturated Fats.** Foods high in saturated fats include cheese, whole milk, ice cream, fatty meats, lard, palm oil, and coconut oil. It is best to keep your intake of these fats low. They tend to raise blood **cholesterol** levels, which can lead to heart disease. Cholesterol is a fatlike substance present in such foods as meat, milk, eggs, poultry, and fish. Cholesterol and fat are not the same thing, but eating either raises blood cholesterol levels.

- **Trans Fatty Acids.** Foods high in trans fatty acids include hard margarines and shortenings. These fats are also found in many fried fast foods, as well as in some bakery products. Trans fatty acids also raise blood cholesterol levels.

- **Unsaturated Fats.** Unlike saturated fats, unsaturated fats, or oils, do not raise blood cholesterol levels. Unsaturated oils are divided into two categories: monounsaturated fats and polyunsaturated fats. Olive, canola, sunflower, and peanut oils are high in monounsaturated fats. They can be eaten in moderate amounts in a healthy diet. Sources of polyunsaturated fats include vegetable oils such as soybean oil, corn oil, cottonseed oil, and many types of nuts. Various types of fish, including salmon, tuna, and mackerel, contain omega-3 polyunsaturated fatty acids. Some evidence suggests that omega-3 acids can be beneficial. They may actually lower the risk of breast cancer and provide protection against heart disease.

Use fats sparingly in your diet. Any type of fat contains twice the calories of the same amount of carbohydrate or protein. The total amount of fat in your diet should not be more than 30 percent of your daily calorie intake. Only 10 percent of your fat calories should come from saturated fat.

Beware!

Some product labels list only the total amount of fat—not the type of fat.

Can you find what percentage of your daily allowance for vitamin C is in a serving of this tomato sauce?

Chapter Two

Vitamins and Minerals

Vitamins are **micronutrients**. Your body needs very small amounts of micronutrients, yet they are crucial for good health. Without them, a number of serious medical problems can develop.

Vitamins are substances that increase the speed and effectiveness of chemical reactions in the body. They are sometimes called the body's **catalysts** because they get things going. Vitamins are essential for growth and development, and they regulate certain cell functions.

Vitamins are not interchangeable. Each is responsible for performing specific tasks in the body. Even if you were missing only one vitamin from your diet, you still might have health problems because your body lacked the vitamin. This situation is often called a **vitamin deficiency**.

The ABCs of Vitamins

Your eyes need vitamin A to function properly.

Different foods contain different vitamins. For example, vegetables, fruits, and fruit juices contain significant amounts of vitamins A and C. Vitamin A is important for good vision. It

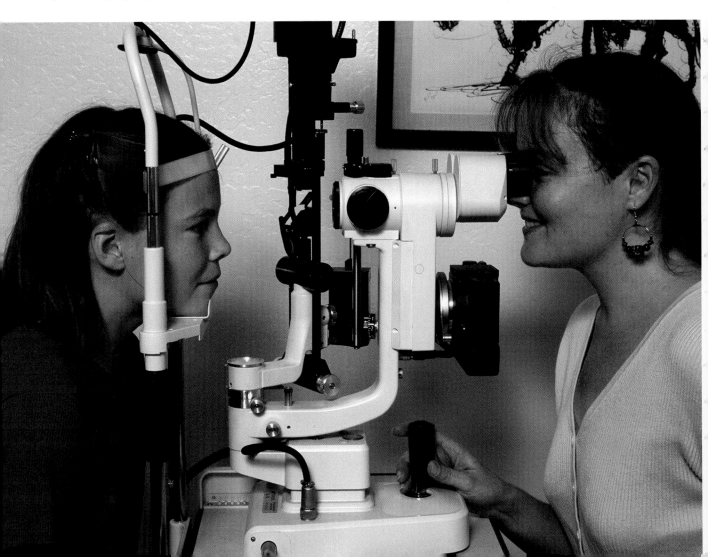

also helps maintain healthy teeth, bones, soft tissues, and skin. In addition, vitamin A is important to the immune system, which protects the body against infection.

Vitamin C is essential for healthy teeth, gums, and bones. It also helps heal injuries and bolsters the body's resistance to infection. Insufficient vitamin C can lead to bleeding gums, swollen joints, slow-healing wounds, bruising, tooth decay, and other problems.

Other essential vitamins include thiamine, or vitamin B_1, vitamin E, and vitamin K. Thiamine is found in cereal, whole grains, fish, meats, dried beans, peas, and soybeans, among other foods. It helps to turn carbohydrates into energy and to maintain healthy nerve cells. Vitamin E is important in the formation of red blood cells. Asparagus, corn, nuts, seeds, spinach, and vegetable oils are good sources of vitamin E. Vitamin K is found in cabbage, cauliflower, kale, and spinach. This vitamin is vital to blood clotting.

A person can get all the vitamins necessary for good health by eating a well-balanced diet. Some people also take vitamin pills to supplement what they eat. Too large a dose of any

*Vitamins help your
body do its work.*

micronutrient can be harmful, however, and may result in serious health problems. It is best to eliminate the need for vitamin supplements through proper nutrition.

Essential Minerals

Like vitamins, minerals are micronutrients. Their job is ensure that the body functions as it should. For example, calcium assists in maintaining teeth and regulating heart function. Good sources of calcium are cheese, yogurt, sardines, collards, turnip greens, oranges, and beans. Magnesium, a mineral found in bananas, green vegetables, corn, apples, and whole-wheat bread, helps to regulate body temperature and bone growth. Zinc aids in healing and fights disease. It is found in beef, lamb, chicken, and sunflower seeds. Potassium is helps to regulate the body's heartbeat. Bananas, peaches, potatoes, avocados, artichokes, white beans, and yogurt contain potassium.

Salt is another important mineral. People need salt to live, but too much of it is very unhealthy. Salt contains sodium, an important substance that helps regulate body fluids

Drinking a glass of milk is a great way to give your body calcium.

21

and blood pressure. Excessive sodium, however, can increase a person's risk for high blood pressure.

U.S. Department of Agriculture research shows that most people in the United States eat too much salt. The majority of healthy adults and children need less than 0.25 teaspoons (1.25 ml) of salt daily. To cut back on your salt intake, try filling your

Processed foods, such as frozen dinners, can be very high in sodium.

salt shaker with a variety of spices and **herbs** instead. These salt substitutes improve the taste of many dishes.

Processed foods, such as frozen dinners, canned soups, bottled sauces, and salad dressings, are often high in sodium. You can check the product information label to see how much sodium an item contains. Look for products with labels that read "low sodium." Foods that are low in salt are low in sodium.

Fruits and vegetables are always good choices if you want to reduce the salt in your diet. These foods are naturally low in sodium. Fresh fish and meat dishes tend to have less salt than most canned or processed forms.

Changing Nutrient Needs

Your nutrient needs change at different times in your life. Most adults over fifty years of age need more calcium than other people. The same is true for teenagers. Studies show that the body's absorption of calcium is greatest during the teen years. Young children, adolescent females, and women of child-bearing age must be sure to get enough of the mineral iron. Cooked dried beans, whole-grain bread, meats, shrimp, clams, and spinach are all good sources of iron. An iron deficiency can result in stunted growth, mental retardation, stillbirths, and other medical conditions.

Food Guide Pyramid
A Guide to Daily Food Choices

Fats, Oils, & Sweets Group
USE SPARINGLY

Meat, Poultry, Fish, Dry Beans, Eggs, & Nuts Group
2–3 SERVINGS

Milk, Yogurt, & Cheese Group
2–3 SERVINGS

Fruit Group
2–4 SERVINGS

Vegetable Group
3–5 SERVINGS

Bread, Cereal, Rice, & Pasta Group
6–11 SERVINGS

Source: U.S. Department of Agriculture; U.S. Department of Health and Human Services

The U.S. Department of Agriculture created the Food Guide Pyramid to help people understand good nutrition.

Chapter Three

The Food Guide Pyramid

Making the best food choices can be challenging. It is unwise to let taste be your only guide. For good health, it is important to eat a balanced diet. The United States Department of Agriculture (USDA) and Department of Health and Human Services (HHS) developed specific guidelines to help people make smarter food choices. These guidelines

Labels Tell a Lot

On labels, ingredients are listed in order according to their weight. The heaviest ingredient is always listed first. So, if the word *water* heads the ingredients list, the product contains more water than anything else.

take the form of a pyramid-shaped chart known as the **Food Guide Pyramid**.

The Food Guide Pyramid is an easy-to-follow plan for a healthy daily diet. It suggests the right amounts to eat of a wide variety of foods from five major food groups. Each group provides some of the nutrients your body requires. Foods from one group cannot replace those from another.

Great Grains

At the base of the pyramid are grains. These foods include breads, cereals, rice, and pasta. In a healthy daily diet, the largest number of servings should come from this group. Grains provide many valuable nutrients and tend to be low in fat. Many grain products are also high in **fiber**. Fiber helps to move food through the body and is therefore important for waste elimination.

Can you identify the different types of grains in this photograph?

When selecting items from this food group, try to pick whole-grain foods. Refined products are lower in fiber and vitamins. To determine which products contain whole grains, check the labeling. Choose foods that list one of the following ingredients first:

- Bulgur (cracked wheat)
- Pearl barley
- Whole oats
- Whole-grain corn
- Oatmeal
- Popcorn
- Whole wheat
- Whole rye

According to the Food Guide Pyramid, you should eat between six and eleven servings of grains every day. That sounds like a lot of food, but it's not. A single serving of grains does not mean a heaping plate of spaghetti, but rather 0.5 cup (124 grams) of spaghetti. Other examples of single servings are one slice of bread, 1 ounce (31 g) of cold cereal, or 0.5 cup (124 g) of rice.

Meeting the food requirement from the grains group can be done easily without overeating. A small bowl of cereal and a slice of toast at breakfast provide two servings. A sandwich at lunch adds two more. An after-school snack of three or four crackers would make up still another serving. A cup of rice or pasta at dinner brings the total up to seven servings. That is already more than the suggested minimum. Although baked goods made from flour, such as cakes and cookies, are in this group, eat them sparingly. Most of these foods offer few nutrients.

Look for Enrichment

Look for the word **enriched** on the labels of pasta and other grains. It indicates that important vitamins and minerals have been added to the product.

According to the Food Guide Pyramid, a piece of bread counts as a serving of grain.

Breakfast Skippers

In the fifth grade, one out of every six students skips breakfast, which is a big mistake. Those who skip breakfast often tend to experience difficulty concentrating and are absent more often. On the other hand, young people who eat breakfast have been shown to be more alert at school and to do better on tests.

Grains are being used creatively to make meals and snacks healthier. Rice has become a low-fat replacement for some high-fat ingredients in candy bars, batter-fried chicken, doughnuts, and dinner mixes. Researchers currently are exploring the cancer-fighting potential of rice. Studies show that rice consumption in the United States is going up at a rate of about 4 percent annually.

Fruit and Vegetables

The fruit and vegetable food groups occupy the second level of the Food Guide Pyramid. Both of these groups play key roles in maintaining good health. The items in these groups are rich in vitamins, minerals, and fiber. Whether fresh, frozen, canned, or dried, fruits and vegetables contain nutrients. The Food Guide Pyramid recommends eating at least two servings of fruits and three servings of vegetables every day.

It is important to vary the fruits and vegetables you eat, as different ones are rich in different nutrients. Kiwi fruits, strawberries, tomatoes, and grapefruits contain vitamin C, as do broccoli, potatoes, and romaine lettuce. Carrots and sweet potatoes are good sources of vitamin A. When choosing your

Try to eat a variety of fruits and vegetables.

fruits and vegetables, remember that color counts. Dark green vegetables and deeply colored fruits are often high in nutrients.

Fruit and vegetable juices contain nutrients as well. If you are choosing between a glass of soda or a glass of juice, the juice is the healthier choice. Whole fruits and vegetables are usually better for you than juices, however. Juices generally contain only a small amount of fiber.

Milk and Meat

The milk group and the meat group occupy the third level of the Food Guide Pyramid. The milk group contains milk, cheese, and yogurt. The meat group consists of red meat, poultry, fish, eggs, cooked dry beans, and nuts. Although nuts and dry beans are included in the meat group, the food on this pyramid level largely comes from animals. It is recommended that you eat two to three servings from each of these groups daily.

When selecting foods from the meat group, some choices are better than others. Always try to pick lean meats and poultry. Remove the skin from chicken and trim off any fat from steaks and chops. It is also wise to limit your intake of high-fat

What's a Sample Serving From the Milk and Meat Group?

Having 1 cup (236 ml) of milk or yogurt equals a serving from the milk group. Eating 2 to 3 ounces (62 to 93 g) of cooked meat, poultry, or fish, which is about the size of a deck of cards, counts as a serving from the meat group. Also, 2 tablespoons (30 ml) of peanut butter—an amount about the size of a Ping-Pong ball—is considered equal to 1 ounce (31 g) of meat.

The milk and the meat group include cheese, nuts, and beef.

Having cereal with low-fat milk is a great way to get a serving of grains as well as a serving from the milk group.

processed meats, such as bologna and salami. Look for low-fat or fat-free varieties, or select lean turkey instead.

Making smart choices from the milk group can make a big difference in your overall health. Choose low-fat or skim varieties of milk. They are lower in saturated fat, while the vitamin and mineral benefits remain the same. Low-fat and fat-free yogurt and cheeses are also healthy choices.

Fats, Oils, and Sweets

The last level of the Food Guide Pyramid is the small tip at the top. It contains foods that should be eaten sparingly. Among them are salad dressings, oils, cream, butter, margarine, sugars, soda, candy, and sweet desserts. Most of these foods are high in calories and offer few health benefits.

In planning your daily diet, start from the bottom of the Food Guide Pyramid and work upward. Get most of your calories from grains, fruits, and vegetables. The fewest calories in your diet should come from the pyramid's tip. Many fancy but fattening desserts look better than they actually taste. Start thinking of a delicious, juicy piece of fruit as the best dessert you could eat.

How Many Calories Should You Have Daily?

1,600 calories—for inactive women and older adults
2,200 calories—for most children, teenage girls, active women, and inactive men
2,800 calories—for teenage boys, most active males, and some extremely active females
(The above calculations are approximations. See your doctor for specific information that applies to you.)

Exercise is an important part of leading a healthy life.

Chapter Four

Get Moving

It is hard to separate a healthy diet from regular exercise. Both are important to maintaining a healthy body and an active lifestyle. Calories that are not used by the body are stored as fat. Physical activity or a daily exercise routine can be an important factor in creating a balance between the number of calories you eat and the number of calories you burn.

Chose Your Fuel Carefully

About 75 percent of the calories your body burns daily are used to supply energy for basic needs, such as breathing, sleeping, digesting food, and moving. If

Are young people on the go? Unfortunately, the answer is no. According to a Surgeon General's report, young people's activity decrease as they advance grade levels. This becomes more dramatic as they enter adolescence. Nearly half of U.S. youths, between 12 and 21 years of age, do not regularly engage in vigorous exercise. Another fourth do not engage in any vigorous activity.

you want to burn more calories than you usually do, you must be more physically active. To lose 1 pound (0.45 kilogram), you have to burn 3,500 more calories than you eat. You can do this by eating the same number of calories and increasing your physical activity. You can also reduce the number of calories you consume while being more active.

If you cut down on calories, it is still important to eat a healthy, balanced diet. These tips will help:

- Eat less fat.
- Bake, broil, or steam foods instead of frying them.
- Eat an English muffin instead of a pastry.
- Drink water instead of soda.
- Eat only half of your dessert. Save the other half for the following day.
- Do not add sugar to cereals or fatty sauces to rice or pasta.
- Eat sorbet, sherbet, or low-fat frozen yogurt instead of ice cream.
- Eat fish, skinless chicken, or turkey more often than red meat.
- Eat low-fat snacks. Baked chips are better than fried ones.

Pick an Activity, any Activity

Obesity, or being very overweight, in both children and adults is on the rise in the United States. Among children and teens, the overall increase in body fat has been linked to more television viewing and spending less time exercising. Ideally, children should engage in one hour of physical activity on most days. Adults need a minimum of about half that amount.

Spending too much time in front of the television is considered to be a leading factor in the increase of obese young people.

Being physically active does not mean you have to join a health club. There are many ways to be active, including canoeing, biking, swimming, jogging, dancing, or cross-country skiing. Team sports are also excellent forms of exercise. You also don't need fancy equipment or special training to increase your physical activity. You don't even need to be especially athletic. You can improve your health and fitness level by simply going for brisk daily walks.

In choosing physical activities, pick things you like to do. People are more likely to continue with activities they enjoy

Learn What You Burn

Activity	Calories Burned Per Hour
Bicycling at 6 miles (9.5 km) per hour	240
Jumping rope	920
Jogging at 5.5 miles (8.8 km) per hour	740
Walking at 2 miles (3.2 km) per hour	400
Playing tennis	500

The above calculations are approximations.

than with an exercise regimen that feels like an unpleasant chore. The best exercise plan is one that you continue to follow over time. To prevent boredom and to exercise different parts of the body, try to vary your activities. Find a few things that are fun for you and rotate them.

Physical activity does more than burn calories. Among other benefits, it reduces the risk of developing a number of illnesses and enhances your general well being. The National Heart, Lung, and Blood Institute, one of the National

Give Your Heart and Lungs a Workout

Swimming, running, and jumping rope are examples of **aerobic** activity. In aerobics, the body uses oxygen to produce the energy necessary for the activity. If done for a half hour at least three times a week, aerobic exercise conditions the heart and lungs.

Exercise doesn't need to be complicated. It can be as simple as taking your dog for a walk.

Institutes of Health, cites the following health benefits as resulting from regular physical activity:

- gives you more energy
- helps in coping with stress
- improves your self-image
- increases resistance to fatigue

- helps counter anxiety and depression
- helps you to relax and feel less tense
- improves your ability to fall asleep quickly and sleep well
- provides an easy way to share an activity with friends or family and an opportunity to meet new friends
- helps you to be more productive at work or school
- increases your capacity for physical work
- builds **stamina** for other physical activities
- increases muscle strength
- helps your heart and lungs work more efficiently

You can also increase your physical activity by being a little more active in your everyday life. If possible, walk or bike to your destinations instead of traveling by car. Take your dog for extra-long walks—it's a healthy habit for both of you. Use the stairs instead of taking the elevator. Wash the family car.

Use some of the time that you might spend watching television or playing computer games in a healthier way. Learn a new dance or take up gardening or roller skating. If you are physically inactive, start slowly. Remember that any physical activity, even if done for only a few minutes a day, is better than none.

A nutritionist works with two young people to help them understand what a healthy diet is and to answer their questions.

Chapter Five

Common Diet Questions

Healthy eating is a broad topic with many facets. This chapter delves into some of the most common questions about eating right.

Question: I know that water is an important nutrient. Does my body need more of it when I exercise?

Answer: It is always important to drink enough water, but this is especially true when exercising. Professional athletes drink water before, during, and after exercising. A good rule to follow is to drink 8 ounces (227 ml) of water before starting and another 8 ounces for every fifteen minutes of intense exercise you do. If you are going outdoors to play sports, jog, or walk, bring along a bottle filled with cold water.

Question: Can sports drinks replace water? Are they good for me?

Answer: Today some people drink sports drinks when exercising. These beverages replace the water and salts that the body loses when it sweats. Sports drinks provide necessary minerals, such as potassium, and some fuel in the form of sugar. Other people, however, prefer to drink only water. They argue that sports drinks contain sodium and sugar, and most Americans already have too much of these substances in their diets. Those favoring water also point out us that water is inexpensive and readily available. Actually, you can safely drink either. The most important thing to remember is always to replace some liquid when exercising.

Question: Is it possible to eat a vegetarian, or meatless, diet and still follow the Food Guide Pyramid recommendations?

Answer: Yes, most vegetarian diets fit into the guidelines. This is especially true for vegetarians who eat eggs and milk products. The necessary protein for a healthy diet does not have to come from meat or fish. Protein is readily available in dry beans, soy products, yogurt, cheese, and other foods.

Vegans are vegetarians who only eat foods from

Vegetarians get protein from sources other than meat. They eat beans, tofu, cheese, and yogurt instead.

plants. Their diets lack vitamin B$_{12}$, which comes only from animal sources. Vegans must be especially careful to get enough calcium and vitamin D, because these nutrients largely come from milk products. Taking a vitamin supplement can fulfill this need.

Eating Trendy?

According to the American Dietetic Association, about one-third of U.S. teens think that being a vegetarian is cool.

Question: Is pasta fattening?

Answer: Eaten in the recommended portions, pasta by itself is not fattening. It is what you put on pasta that can make it a high-calorie food. When eating pasta, cut down on fatty sauces, such as cream-based ones. Use tomato-based sauces instead. Garlic, herbs, and low-fat cheeses can spice up a portion of pasta as well without adding a large number of calories.

Question: I seem to have a natural sweet tooth. Was I born loving cake and candy?

Answer: Research shows that all babies are born with a preference for sweets. At about four months old, they also develop a preference for salt. This does not mean that sweet and salty foods have to dominate your diet, however. You can enjoy them in reasonable portions.

Question: Are fad diets, such as the cabbage soup diet, the grapefruit diet, liquid diets, and high-protein diets, any good?

Answer: Fad diets frequently center around one food or one type of food. The majority of these eating plans are based

What you put on your pasta and how much of it you eat can make it a fattening food.

A young woman reads the label of a liquid diet product. It is better to eat real meals than to rely on any special products.

on drastically cutting calories and depriving your body of valuable nutrients. In many cases, this actually triggers overeating, making it even harder to maintain weight loss over an extended period. The American Dietetic Association cites the following as among the "red flags" that signal poor nutrition advice or fad diet claims:

- claims that sound too good to be true
- simple conclusions drawn from complex studies
- dramatic promises that are refuted by reputable scientific groups
- lists of "good" and "bad" foods

Remember, there are no magical foods that bring about weight loss. The best thing to do is to eat appropriately and to exercise.

Question: As long as I eat the right foods, does portion size really matter that much?

Answer: Portion size is crucial in maintaining a healthy weight. It is also important not to eat too much of one or two foods and leave out others that can provide important nutrients. Check the Nutrition Facts label to learn how much food equals a single serving. If you are served a very large meal when eating out, take half of it home. At many restaurants, two people can share an entrée or a dessert. It is especially important to limit portion size when eating high-calorie foods such as cakes, cookies, and french fries.

Question: Are herbal diet drugs safe because they are made of natural substances?

Answer: Herbal weight-loss products carry numerous risks. Many contain a substance called **ephedra**. Overdoses of ephedra can cause changes in heart rhythm, seizures, and an increase in blood pressure. In the 1990s, several deaths and serious medical complications were linked to ephedra use.

Question: When does a healthy interest in nutrition turn out to be an eating disorder?

Answer: The signs of a serious eating disorder include the following:

- frequent episodes of uncontrolled or binge eating. The binges may or may not be followed by varying periods of fasting or severely restricted eating
- a preoccupation with the amounts and types of foods eaten
- a preoccupation with weight and body image
- a dramatic and often unhealthy weight loss
- an excessive exercise regime
- self-induced vomiting after meals and snacks
- **laxative** abuse

People with eating disorders often have a poor self-image. They see themselves as overweight even when they are slender.

Two of the best-known eating disorders are anorexia and bulimia. Anorexics starve themselves and usually weigh about 15 percent less than a healthy body weight. Although anorexics can be extremely thin, they are convinced that they are overweight. People who are bulimic experience episodes of binge eating. These are followed by a need to "purge" the food. Methods of purging include vomiting, fasting, enema use, excessive laxative use, and compulsive exercise. Bulimics are obsessed with not gaining weight. Unlike anorexics, however, they are usually of about normal weight.

Question: There's been a lot of talk about safety in food preparation. Does food have to be cooked to a certain temperature to be safe?

Answer: Animal food products that are improperly cooked can be unsafe. When preparing meat and egg dishes, using a food thermometer is the best way to tell if the food is cooked to the right temperature. Follow these food-safety tips:

To avoid food-borne illnesses, make sure that your food is cooked to the right temperature.

- Always reheat sauces, soups, and gravies to a boil. Leftovers should be heated to a temperature of 165° Fahrenheit (73.8° Celsius).
- Don't eat raw or partially cooked eggs. They may contain bacteria that cause salmonella poisoning. Salmonella poisoning can lead to very serious health problems. Both egg yolks and whites should be cooked until firm.
- Ask that foods be well cooked when eating out and insist that they be served piping hot.
- Pay close attention to the safety instructions on food packaging. Following instructions, such as "keep refrigerated" or "close tightly," can be extremely important in preventing food poisoning.
- Always check the expiration dates on products such as milk, cheese, yogurt, and other **perishable** items.

Timeline

1862	The United States Department of Agriculture (USDA) is created.
1865	Pasteurization, a process through which bacteria in milk is destroyed, is invented by French chemist Louis Pasteur.
1888	Refrigerated train boxcars make possible the first long-haul shipments of meats, fruits, and vegetables.
1906	The first Pure Food and Drug Act is passed. This legislation is designed to prevent the manufacture and sale of spoiled, mislabeled, or poisonous foods or drugs.
1915	Vitamin C is discovered.
1922	Vitamin E is discovered.
1939	Vitamin K is discovered.
1941	The USDA publishes its first guide for healthy daily nutrition.
1954	Frozen foods become widely available. For the first time, a wide range of foods are available during every season of the year.
1960s	High-protein and protein-only fad diets become popular. Some people suffer liver and kidney damage as a result.
1974	The Safe Drinking Water Act is passed to protect the quality of drinking water in the United States.
1992	The USDA releases the Food Guide Pyramid.
1994	Take-out food accounts for more than 30 percent of the average American family's food budget.
1997	The USDA overhauls the School Lunch Program, requiring that school meals meet dietary guidelines for healthy living. The School Lunch Program provides low-cost lunches to more than 25 million children.

Glossary

aerobic—describing an activity in which the body uses oxygen to produce the necessary energy

amino acids—natural substances that are the building blocks of proteins

antibodies—bodily substances that fight infection and disease

calories—the units in which the energy various foods contain is measured

carbohydrate—a macronutrient that provides energy and is found in foods, such as bread and rice

catalyst—a substance that speeds up or causes a chemical reaction

cholesterol—a fatlike substance present in foods, such as whole milk, eggs, poultry, and fish

dehydration—a dangerous depletion of body fluids

digestion—the process of breaking down food in the body so that it can be absorbed into the bloodstream

enriched—containing added vitamins and minerals

enzyme—a protein that speeds up important chemical reactions in the body

ephedra—an ingredient that is used in some diet pills and can have deadly side effects

evaporate—when a liquid becomes a gas or vapor

fat—a macronutrient found in foods, such as meat, milk, and nuts. Fat stores energy and helps keep you warm.

fiber—a part of foods that passes through the body undigested. Fiber assists in elimination by helping to move food through the body.

Food Guide Pyramid—a pyramid-shaped chart that contains guidelines for a healthy diet

grain—a type of plant

herb—a plant used to flavor food or for medical purposes

hormones—substances in the body that regulate important processes such as growth and development

laxative—a substance taken to relieve constipation

legumes—plants that grow in pods, such as peas, beans, and peanuts

macronutrients—four substances—water, carbohydrates, proteins, and fats—that are needed in large amounts for good health

micronutrients—the vitamins and minerals in foods that are necessary for good health

nutrients—substances in food that are necessary for good health

obesity—the condition of being very overweight

perishable—likely to spoil quickly

processed foods—foods that have been treated or prepared by a special method

protein—a macronutrient found in foods, such as meat, cheese, and beans, that helps the body function

Recommended Daily Allowance—the correct amount of a nutrient that most people need in a day

stamina—strength and endurance

vegan—a person who only eats foods that come from plants

vitamin—a substance in food that increases the speed of vital chemical reactions in the body

vitamin deficiency—to lack the proper amount of a vitamin or certain vitamins needed for good health

To Find
Out More

Books

Christian, Rebecca. *Cooking the Spanish Way*. Minneapolis, MN: Lerner, 2000.

Duden, Jane. *Vegetarianism for Teens*. Mankato, MN: Capstone Press, 2001.

Gaby, Jackie. *The Giant Book of the Body*. Brookfield, CT: Millbrook Press, 2000.

Hughes, Meredith Sayles. *Spill the Beans and Pass the Peanuts: Legumes*. Minneapolis, MN: Lerner, 1999.

Luby, Thia. *Yoga For Teens: How To Improve Your Fitness, Confidence, Appearance, and Health—and Have Fun Doing It*. Santa Fe, NM: Clear Light, 2000.

Marshall, Elizabeth L. *High-Tech Harvest*. Danbury, CT: Franklin Watts, 1999.

Matthews, Rupert. *Cooking a Meal*. Danbury, CT: Franklin Watts, 2000.

Sneddon, Pamela Shires. *Body Image: A Reality Check*. Berkeley Heights, NJ: Enslow, 1999.

Turck, Mary. *Healthy Eating For Weight Management*. Mankato, MN: Capstone Press, 2001.

Yancey, Diane. *Eating Disorders*. Brookfield, CT: Twenty-First Century Books, 1999.

Yu, Ling. *Cooking the Chinese Way*. Minneapolis, MN: Lerner, 2002.

Zanger, Mark H. *The American Ethnic Cookbook for Students*. Phoenix, AR: ORYX, 2001.

Organizations and Online Sites

Center for Nutrition Policy and Promotion, USDA
1120 20th Street NW, Suite 200, North Lobby
Washington, DC 20036
http://www.usda.gov/cnpp
This site is a good source of information on the nutrient content of food and dietary guidelines.

Food and Nutrition Information Center

National Agricultural Library, USDA

10301 Baltimore Boulevard, Room 304

Beltsville, MD 20705-2351

http://www.nal.usda.gov/fnic/

The National Agricultural Library (NAL) is a major source of information about agriculture and nutrition.

Healthfinder

National Health Information Center

U.S. Department of Health and Human Services

P.O. Box 1133

Washington, DC 20012-1133

http://www.healthfinder.gov

This online site contains health information from A to Z. Don't miss the special section for kids and teens.

Food Safety and Inspection Service

Food Safety Education Staff

1400 Independence Avenue SW

Room 2942S

Washington, DC 20250

http://www.fsis.usda.gov

This site provides everything you need to know about food safety. There is a fun educational section for young people as well.

Food and Drug Administration
200 C Street SW
Washington, DC 20204
http://www.fda.gov
You'll find reliable information about foodborne illnesses, nutrition, and dietary supplements here. The online site also contains an inviting information page for young people.

Centers for Disease Control and Prevention
1600 Clifton Road
Atlanta, GA 30333
http://www.cdc.gov
This site covers a large number of health topics, including disease prevention and nutrition.

A Note on Sources

A variety of sources were helpful in doing the research for this book. These included numerous publications from the U.S. Department of Agriculture and the Institute of Agriculture and Natural Resources at the University of Nebraska (Cooperative Extension).

The National Heart, Lung, and Blood Institute publication, "Exercise and Your Health: A Guide To Physical Activity" was also helpful. Still more valuable information came from the report on the symposium on childhood obesity presented by the Center for Nutrition Policy and Promotion. Various periodicals proved useful in my research as well. Among these were the magazines *Food Technology* and *Pediatric Nursing*.

In many instances, the online sites of a number of highly reliable institutions offered timely dietary data. The following organizations were excellent sources for the latest facts and figures: American Dietetic Association, University of California, Davis School of Medicine and Medical Center, Heart Information Network, American Heart Association, and National Institutes of Health—Medline Plus.

—*Elaine Landau*

Index

Numbers in *italics* indicate illustrations.

About the Author

Popular author Elaine Landau worked as a newspaper reporter, editor, and youth services librarian before becoming a full-time writer. She has written more than two hundred nonfiction books for young people. She has written many books for Franklin Watts on health topics, including *Autism*, *Tourette Syndrome*, and *Parkinson's Disease*. Ms. Landau, who has a bachelor's degree in English and journalism from New York University and a master's degree in library and information science from Pratt Institute, lives in Florida.